THE SCIENCE BEHIND
SUPERMAN'S
SIGHT

DC SUPER HEROES

by
Agnieszka Biskup

Superman created by
Jerry Siegel and Joe Shuster
by special arrangement with
the Jerry Siegel family

SCIENCE BEHIND
SUPERMAN

CAPSTONE PRESS
a capstone imprint

Published by Capstone Press in 2017
A Capstone Imprint
1710 Roe Crest Drive
North Mankato, Minnesota 56003
www.mycapstone.com

STAR38175

Library of Congress Cataloging-in-Publication Data
Names: Biskup, Agnieszka, author.
Title: The science behind Superman's sight / by Agnieszka Biskup.
Description: North Mankato, Minnesota : Capstone Press, 2016. | Series: DC super heroes.
   Science behind Superman | Audience: Ages 7-9. | Audience: K to grade 3. | Includes bibliographical
   references and index.
Identifiers: LCCN 2016033218 (print) | LCCN 2016040873 (ebook) | ISBN 9781515750987 (library binding) |
   ISBN 9781515751021 (paperback) | ISBN 9781515751144 (eBook PDF)
Subjects: LCSH: Vision—Juvenile literature. | Eye—Juvenile literature. | Superman (Fictitious character)—
   Juvenile literature.
Classification: LCC QP475.7 .B56 2016 (print) | LCC QP475.7 (ebook) | DDC 612.8/4—dc23
LC record available at https://lccn.loc.gov/2016033218

Summary
Explores the science behind Superman's eyesight and describes examples of sight from the real world.

Editorial Credits
Aaron Sautter, editor; Veronica Scott, designer; Kelly Garvin, media researcher;
Katy LaVigne, production specialist

Photo Credits
Capstone Press: Erik Doescher, cover, backcover, 1, 3, Luciano Vecchio, 6, 9 (top), 11, 12, 15, 21, Mike Cavallaro,
5, 18, Min Sung Ku, 22; Newscom: Cristobal Garcia/EPA, 17, Staff/MCT, 16; Shutterstock: AkeSak, 14, (inset),
Designua, 7 (t), 8, Ivan Smuk, 19, MilanB, 7 (bottom), Peter Hermes Furian, 9 (b), Romaset, 13, Tim UR, 10, wang
song, 20, wavebreakmedia, 14

Printed and bound in the USA.
010023S17

Table of Contents

INTRODUCTION
Amazing Eyes 4

CHAPTER 1
Seeing the Light 6

CHAPTER 2
Improving Vision 12

CHAPTER 3
Going Beyond Our Limits 18

GLOSSARY 22

INTERNET SITES 23

READ MORE 23

INDEX 23

AMAZING EYES

Superman is known for his super-strength.
But his super-vision is just as incredible.
He has **X-ray** vision, heat vision, microscopic
vision, and more. People don't have the
Man of Steel's powers. But the science behind
sight is still amazing.

FACT
Superman was first shown using
X-ray vision in comics in 1939. He
began using heat vision in 1949.

X-ray—an invisible high-energy beam of light that can pass
through solid objects

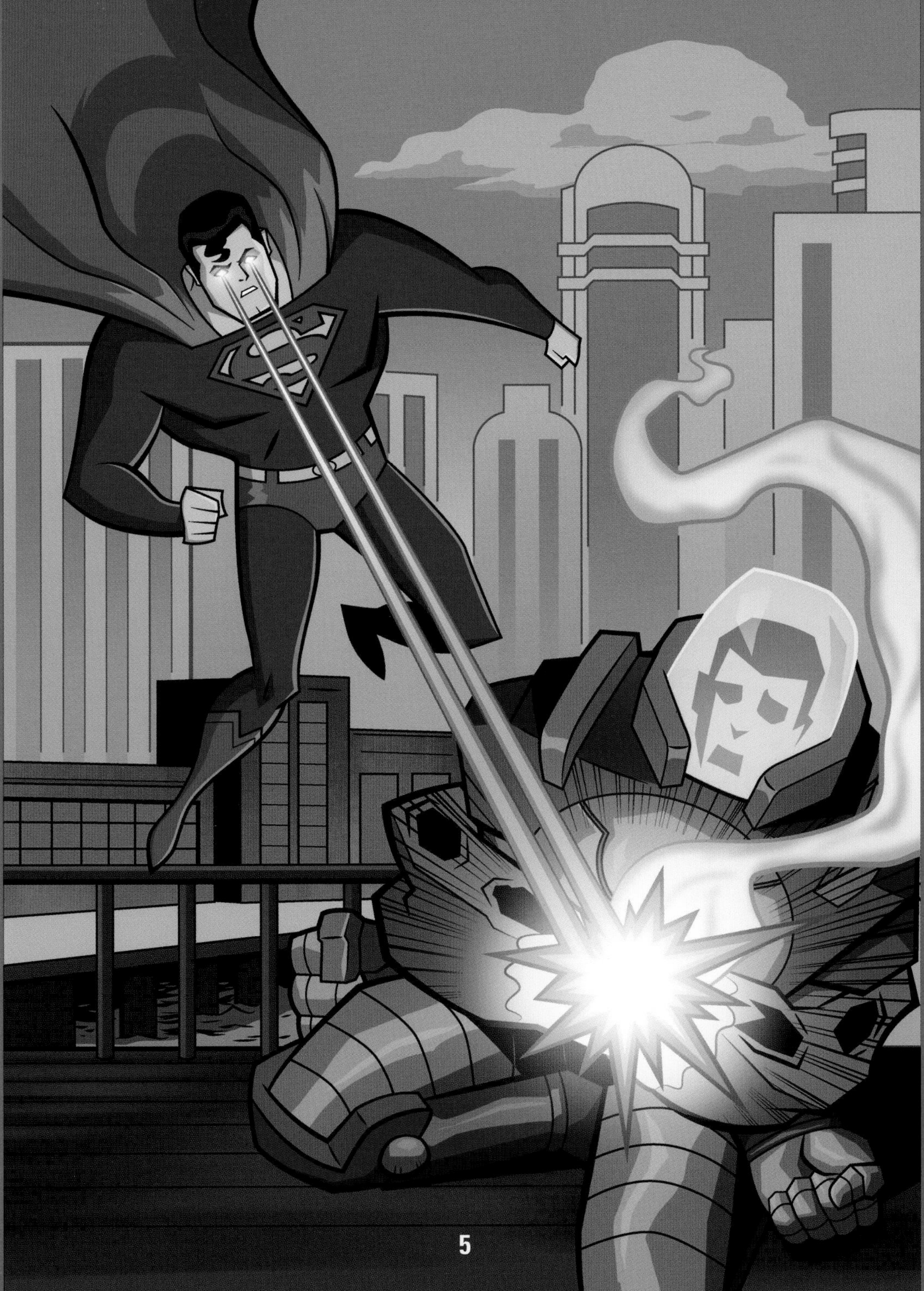

CHAPTER 1

SEEING THE LIGHT

Human sight is almost as amazing as Superman's powers. The science of sight begins with light. Visible light is part of the **electromagnetic spectrum**. This spectrum also includes energy waves we can't see like X-rays, **ultraviolet light**, and radio waves.

electromagnetic spectrum—the range of frequencies of electromagnetic radiation from gamma rays to visible light to radio waves

ultraviolet light—an invisible form of light that can cause sunburns

THE ELECTROMAGNETIC SPECTRUM

Radio waves | Micro-waves | Infrared radiation | Visible light | Ultraviolet | X-rays | Gamma-rays

10^3 1 10^{-3} 10^{-5} 10^{-7} 10^{-9} 10^{-11} 10^{-13}

FACT

White light isn't really white. It's a combination of all the colors. A prism can split white light into its separate colors. These include red, orange, yellow, green, blue, indigo, and violet.

Vision depends on the eyes' ability to detect light energy. Light reflects off objects. It then enters our eyes and lands on the retinas. The retina has light **sensitive** cells called rods and cones. These cells help us see different colors and levels of light.

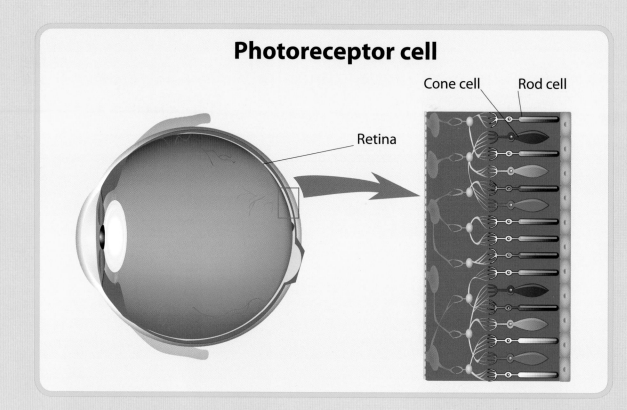

Photoreceptor cell

Cone cell   Rod cell

Retina

sensitive—able to detect or react to the slightest change in something

eye lens

retina

FACT

Your eyes' lenses create upside down and backward images on the retinas. Your brain then flips the images back to tell you what you see.

People can't see through walls like Superman. However, we can see about one million different colors. How? Our eyes work with reflected light to see color. For example, a ripe apple reflects the red **wavelength** of light. The cone cells in our eyes then send signals to our brains, which tell us we are seeing red.

FACT

Some people are color blind. Most color blind people can't tell the difference between red and green colors. A small number of people can't see color at all.

wavelength—the distance between two peaks of a wave

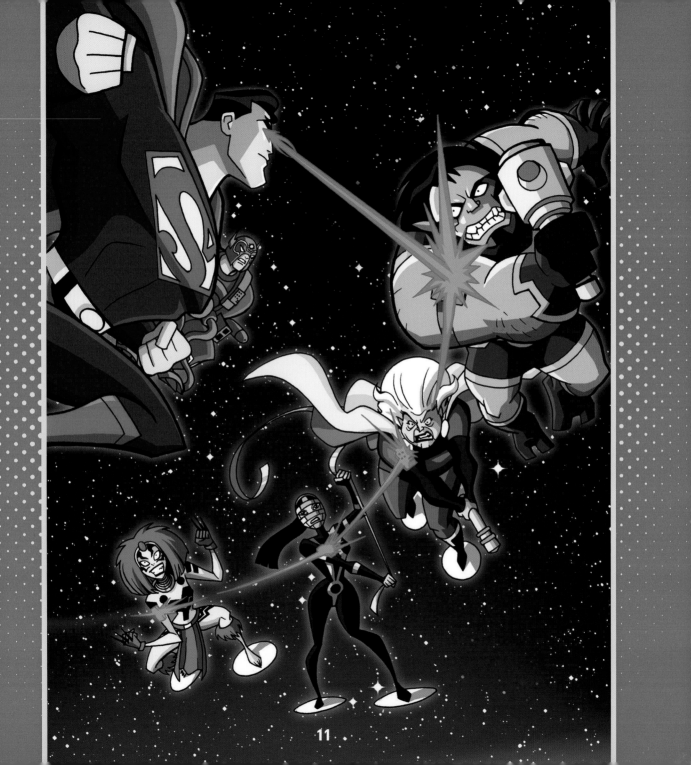

CHAPTER 2

IMPROVING VISION

Clark Kent wears glasses, but he doesn't need them to see. However, many people do need glasses. The lenses in their eyes don't work correctly. Some glasses have **concave** lenses. They help nearsighted people see faraway objects. Glasses with **convex** lenses help farsighted people see up-close objects better.

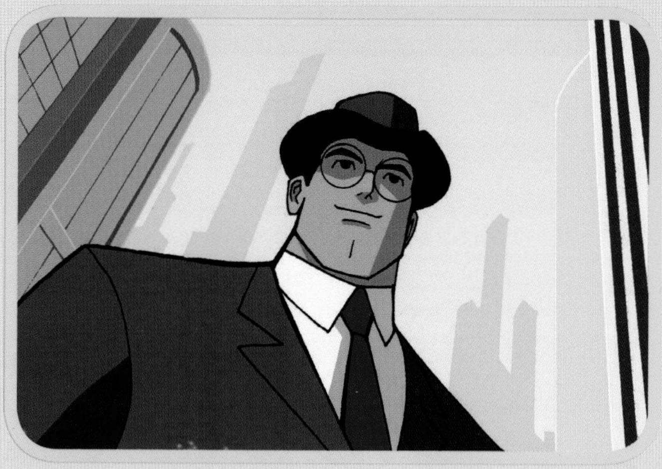

concave—a surface that is hollow and curved, like the inside of a bowl
convex—a surface that curves outward, like the outside of a ball

FACT

Some people choose laser eye surgery to correct their vision. Surgeons use lasers to carefully reshape their eyes. Afterward, most people no longer need glasses to see clearly.

Superman can see tiny objects that human eyes can't. But people can see them using microscopes. Microscopes use lenses to **magnify** objects that are too small to see. Doctors use microscopes to look at blood and tissue samples. Scientists use them to study plant and animal cells.

human cells

Electron microscopes use beams of electrons to create detailed images of the tiniest things. These powerful microscopes can magnify objects a million times or more!

magnify—to make something look larger than it really is

Superman can see objects clearly from miles away. But people use telescopes to see over great distances. **Refracting** telescopes work like microscopes. They use curved lenses to make distant objects look closer. A reflecting telescope uses a large curved mirror to gather light. The light is reflected into the telescope's eyepiece.

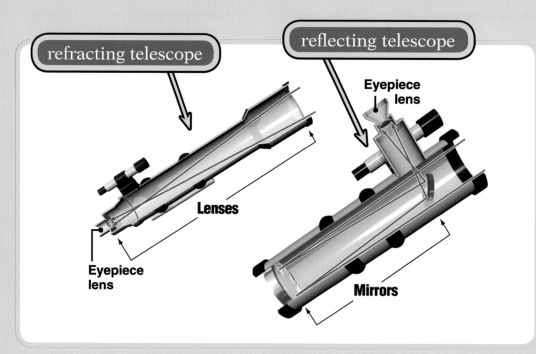

refracting telescope

reflecting telescope

Eyepiece lens

Lenses

Eyepiece lens

Mirrors

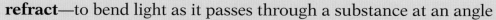

refract—to bend light as it passes through a substance at an angle

The Great Canary Telescope is the world's largest telescope. Its mirror spans 34.1 feet (10.4 meters) across.

CHAPTER 3

GOING BEYOND OUR LIMITS

Superman can melt icebergs with his heat vision. But people use another version of heat vision. Thermal imaging equipment detects **infrared light** waves, which carry heat. Thermal cameras change the invisible heat waves into light that people can see. The cameras see the heat given off by people, animals, and other objects.

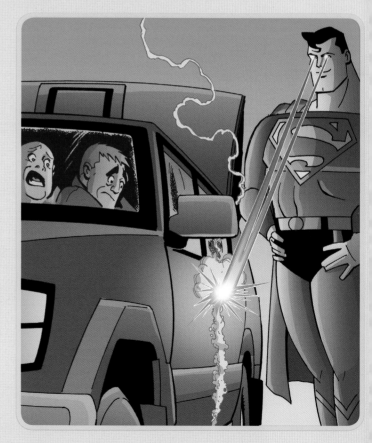

Thermal cameras are often used by firefighters, the military, and police officers. The cameras can help find people in dark or smoky areas.

infrared light—an invisible form of light that gives off heat

Superman's most famous power of sight is his X-ray vision. Doctors often use X-ray images to find and treat injuries. X-ray waves pass right through skin and muscle. But dense bone blocks most of the waves. Bones show up as white in the image. This allows doctors to easily see where a bone may be broken.

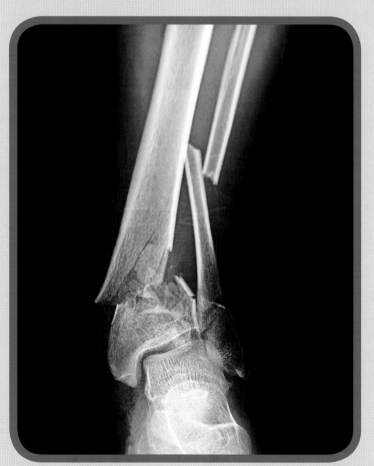

Today researchers are working on ways to enhance human sight. **Bionic** eyes can help blind people see. Special contact lenses help people zoom in their vision. Perhaps one day, humans may have amazing powers of sight just like Superman.

bionic—relating to mechanical replacement body parts

GLOSSARY

bionic (bye-ON-ik)—relating to mechanical replacement body parts

concave (kahn-KAYV)—a surface that is hollow and curved, like the inside of a bowl

convex (kahn-VEKS)—a surface that curves outward, like the outside of a ball

electromagnetic spectrum (i-lek-troh-mag-NET-ik SPEK-truhm)—the range of frequencies of electromagnetic radiation from gamma rays to visible light to radio waves

infrared light (IN-fruh-red LITE)—an invisible form of light that gives off heat

magnify (MAG-nih-fye)—to make something look larger than it really is

refract (ree-FRAKT)—to bend light as it passes through a substance at an angle

sensitive (SEN-suh-tiv)—able to detect or react to the slightest change in something

ultraviolet light (uhl-truh-VYE-uh-lit LITE)—an invisible form of light that can cause sunburns

wavelength (WAYV-length)—the distance between two peaks of a wave

X-ray (EKS-ray)—an invisible high-energy beam of light that can pass through solid objects

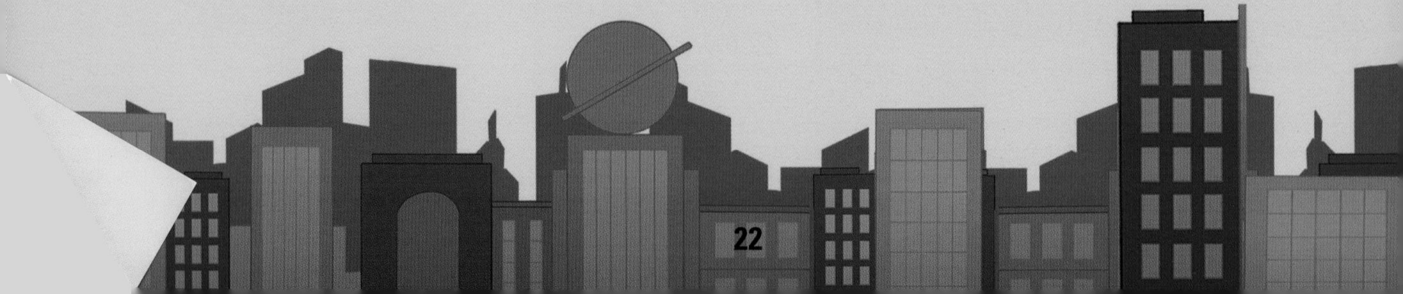

READ MORE

Loria, Laura. *The Eyes in Your Body.* Let's Find Out! The Human Body. New York: Britannica Educational Publishing, 2015.

Slike, Janet. *Take a Closer Look at Your Eyes.* Mankato, Minn.: Child's World, 2013.

Spilsbury, Louise and Richard. *Light and Dark.* Exploring Light. Chicago: Heinemann Raintree, 2016.

INTERNET SITES

FactHound offers a safe, fun way to find Internet sites related to this book. All of the sites on FactHound have been researched by our staff.

Here's all you do:
Visit *www.facthound.com*
Type in this code: 9781515750987

INDEX

bionic eyes, 21
brains, 9, 10

color, 8, 10
color blindness, 10
contact lenses, 21

electromagnetic
   spectrum, 6

eyes, 8, 9, 12, 14
   cones, 8, 10
   lenses, 9, 12
   retinas, 8, 9
   rods, 8

glasses, 12, 13

laser eye surgery, 13

light, 6, 7, 8, 10, 18

microscopes, 14, 15, 16

telescopes, 16, 17
thermal cameras, 18, 19

X-rays, 6, 20

READ THEM ALL!

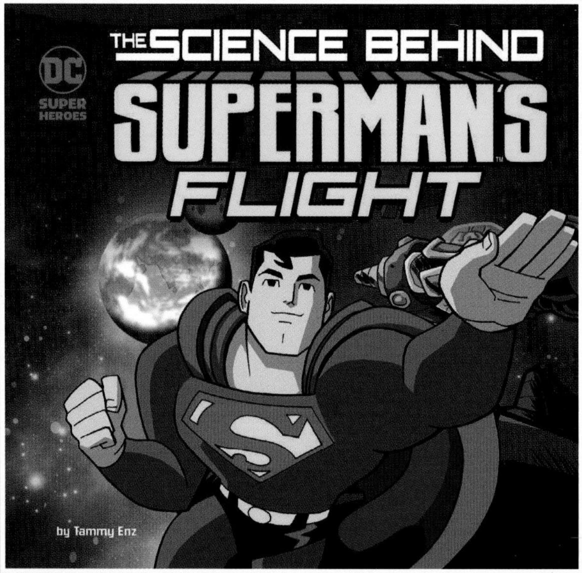
DC
SUPER HEROES
THE SCIENCE BEHIND
SUPERMAN'S
FLIGHT
by Tammy Enz

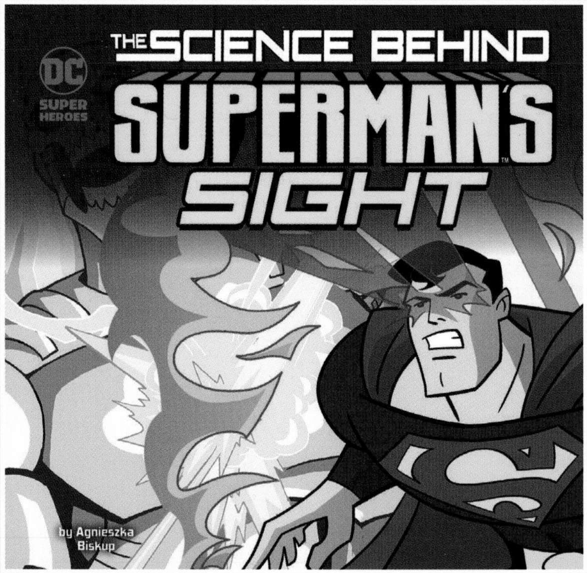
DC
SUPER HEROES
THE SCIENCE BEHIND
SUPERMAN'S
SIGHT
by Agnieszka Biskup

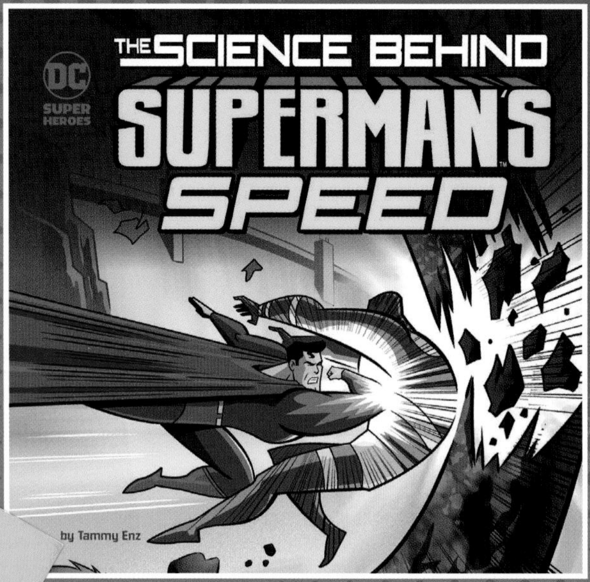
DC
SUPER HEROES
THE SCIENCE BEHIND
SUPERMAN'S
SPEED
by Tammy Enz

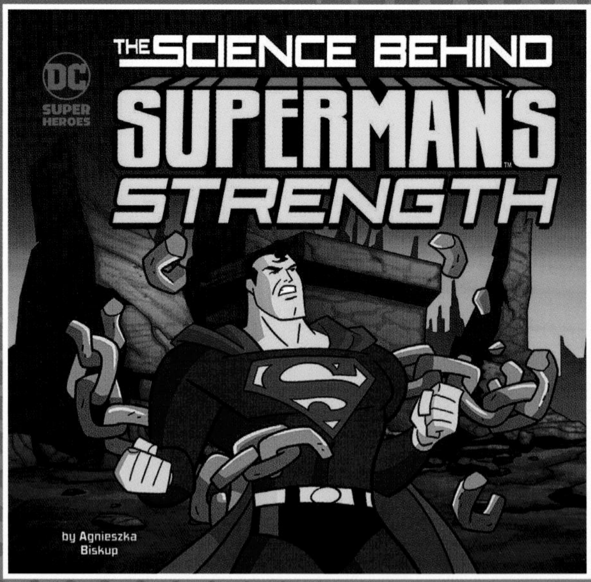
DC
SUPER HEROES
THE SCIENCE BEHIND
SUPERMAN'S
STRENGTH
by Agnieszka Biskup